THE BLUFFER'S GUIDES

BLUFF YOUR WAY IN
BRITISH CLASS

PETER GAMMOND

RAVETTE BOOKS

Published by Ravette Books Limited
Egmont House
8 Clifford Street
London W1X 1RB
(071) 734 0221

First printed 1986
Reprinted 1990, 1992, 1993

Series Editor – Anne Tauté

Designer – Jim Wire
Printer – Cox & Wyman Ltd.

The Bluffer's Guides® is a
Registered Trademark.

The Bluffer's Guides series is based
on an original idea by Peter Wolfe.

An Oval Project
Produced by Oval Projects Ltd. for
Ravette Books, an Egmont company.

CONTENTS

INTRODUCTION

There is a misguided tendency today to try to minimise the validity and effect of Class. There are even some, writing in their heavily class-orientated newspapers and journals, who would have one believe that Britain is moving toward a classless society; that the class system no longer has the significance it once had.

You must not believe a word of this. The old established class system is very much alive and kicking and as virulent as ever. In fact, the subject of class, in some barely disguised form or other, is the country's (and even the world's) favourite topic of conversation. It is discussed at least once a day somewhere on radio and television.

Possibly the dividing lines are rather more blurred than they were. But that is only because people are ever more frantically concerned with blurring them in their efforts to move up (or appear to have moved up) a class beyond their natural station.

The young, in particular, go in for wholesale blurring with their constant wish to style themselves in a standard manner. But to the knowledgeable observer, class can even imprint itself upon a pair of blue jeans. And once the adolescent craving for uniformity has passed, it is remarkable how suddenly and completely the young adults of the species take on the accepted plumage of their rightful category.

The broad-minded (who are really very bigotted) may well say: What does it matter? Yet just how much it matters is apparent in every perceivable manifestation of human behaviour.

Class is therefore a field particularly open to the bluffer. It is the preserve of the true double, and even on occasions, the triple bluff. However, to be effective in these areas you must, in the first place, know where you belong. Otherwise you will not really know where you are trying not to be, and where you are trying to make someone believe you are.

What of those who were at the Last Supper?
Were they Lower or Middle or Upper?

And what of the offspring of Noah?
Were they Middle or Upper or Lower?

And Adam and Eve – there's a riddle.
Were they Upper or Lower or Middle?

A QUICK GUIDE TO THE CLASSES

At one time the simple divisions of Upper, Middle and Lower were considered adequate to define class structure. But such is the complexity of modern life that it is now necessary for each stratum itself to be divided into Upper, Middle and Lower, as follows:

Upper Upper Class
Middle Upper Class
Lower Upper Class

Upper Middle Class
Middle Middle Class
Lower Middle Class

Upper Lower Class
Middle Lower Class
Lower Lower Class

The point of acquiring class is that it gives one power and precedence over the class below; and conversely, the acquisition of power, provided it is supported by a clean sheet (i.e. no *known* shady dealings in the process of acquiring it), can move a person up a class or two. This is known as uppance.

You will have to be very honest with yourself if you are going to fix your Class accurately. Generally speaking the middle level of each class can be taken as its solid and typical core while the Upper and Lower layers are the escape routes for those in transit.

Upper Upper Class

The true (or landed) Upper Class is a very small section of society. It is made up of people who can trace their family tree back to William the Conqueror (beyond whom it is neither advisable nor profitable to go) and have inherited titles or properties of historical standing; the peers of the realm. They used to be able to chop people's heads off but now simply hold on to the aura of having once been able to do it.

By special right the Royal Family are included here (although their quite recent ancestors were foreigners) as they have undeniably lengthy genealogical trees and own lots of genuine castles. With a naturalness that comes of centuries of practice they set the standards and patterns of Upper Upper Class behaviour, speech and dress. Neither Royalty nor the genuine Upper Class ever have to strive for effect. A simple wave of the hand confirms that they are chosen creatures.

It is essential today, in the identification of this species, not to be fooled by the mere possession of a title like Lord. A Lord could easily be of Lower Class strain and simply a friend of a discredited Prime Minister. But you may take it that Dukes are generally acceptable.

Middle Upper Class

Again, quite a small section, but one where the blurring begins. While it is not possible to become Upper Upper Class in much less than a thousand years, it is possible to become Middle Upper Class by:

a)   the faultless acquisition of Upper Class manners

b) popular acclaim
c) self-conviction.

Never, however, simply by the acquisition of wealth. Money cannot buy class; though it can borrow it on a short-term basis at a high rate of interest. Wealth is more influential in the United States and other corrupt foreign countries.

Some less well-established (a hundred years or so) Lords belong to the Middle Upper Class but it is mostly occupied by people whom power has elevated, but not visibly corrupted. Those who achieve such a high stratum as Middle Upper Class may include:

a) Judges (who can send anyone down who is less than their equal)
b) high-ranking Conservative politicians, and statesmen (no other party members can qualify)
c) some top-ranking Service people such as Field-Marshals and Admirals of the Fleet (but not all)
d) some lesser Admirals and Generals provided they have impeccable family backgrounds (but not RAF).

Such people have become so used to power that their natures have changed sufficiently to obscure their origins. It helps to get this high, of course, if you start fairly near the top.

Lower Upper Class

This particular class within a class begins to get a bit more crowded. It includes all those Judges, Conservative politicians and high-ranking military men who have blemishes; which is a considerable percentage. It might today include middle-of-the-road or even left-wing politicians; but mainly those who have renounced titles (see Slumming). It can include assorted Lords and Sirs, and the feminine equivalent (see Marriage – Class by), who have risen to the top through financial acumen, without anyone having discovered how they did it. It can also include high-ranking Civil Servants who have done nothing particularly worthy of the notice of the Press, and other administrators who have wielded ineffective power (Governor-Generals of remote islands, etc.). Even an occasional Archbishop could become Lower Upper Class. Go back a hundred years, or even less, and you would find that almost all political leaders were Upper Class as a matter of course. But today even Conservative leaders can be of quite inferior strain and clearly Middle Class, dependent entirely on the acquisition of the statutory Rt. Hon. to give them credence.

Urban movement has been a great leveller. The Upper Classes used to have Town *and* Country houses. Now comparatively few Upper Class people have Town houses or actually *live* in places like London. Nearly all the large houses in Mayfair are currently utilised as offices or clubs. Upper Class life predominantly flourishes in the country in substantial properties, preferably with stabling, though often in a deplorable state of repair. The rewards of staying in the Upper Class echelons are not necessarily worth the effort. Having to eat pheasant and salmon when you prefer chicken and chips is a bit of a strain in every way.

The **Upper Class** see themselves as the protectors of the proper order of things, upholders of justice, property and relics; the rightful recipients (a reward for natural leadership), of any privileges that may be going.

They see themselves as the 'backbone of Britain'.

Upper Middle Class

These are mainly people who think they are Lower Upper Class but whose flaws are a bit too obvious; perhaps a slight trace of regional accent (this does not apply to Scots or other foreigners) or the inability to choose the right tie, or distinguish real pearls from imitation. In fact, imperfection is almost the trademark of the Upper Middle Class who are an uncomfortable and socially stateless lot. They tend to have got where they are by the entirely unlaudable preoccupation of proving themselves better than the rest of the Middle Class. They will often have yachts that are blatantly larger than some of those possessed by the Lower Upper Class – which is quite unforgiveable – and they live in houses which are too big for comfort.

This category includes the traditional types who entered the Army or the Church because their families could not think of anything better for them to do, in view of limited intellectual capacities or poor commercial prospects.

The Upper Middle Class walk a tightrope between affluence and disaster. They are the filling in the class sandwich, and nobody loves them.

Middle Middle Class

After Upper Upper Class, Middle Middle Class is the best of all categories to be in because it is made up of people who feel totally assured of their role in life.

This section contains a wide cross-section of professions and trades but especially those who have got where they are not by having talent, or by hard work, but by having a good family background.

The Middle Middle Class are the guardians of 'middle-class morality'. Indeed the linking of the two is now almost automatic; presumably based on the assumption that morality is a rather dull business and the other classes have something more interesting to keep them occupied. The Class includes:

a) a fair sprinkling of dons, well-beloved old headmasters, and housemasters

b) service officers above the rank of Major, or its equivalent. (A few Captains are eligible though many of these have acquired the rank as a term of affection or as a figment of their own imagination.)

c) those survivors of the good old days who have what used to be termed 'independent means' or a private income – generally deriving from a few shares in a meat-packing company in Argentina.

d) the 'learned' professions – lawyers, doctors, etc. (but not dentists)

e) respectable areas of fraud such as estate-agency, broking and insurance.

Steady success in a small family business is generally acceptable, particularly where the product is eccentric or specialised. The careful use of categorical descriptions like 'on the Stock Exchange', 'in property dealing' or 'company director' (which can mean anything) have been known to help people get accepted in this privileged section of society. It is the one class where true respectability, or an appearance of it, is more or less essential; and a good school and a 3rd class degree at Oxford or Cambridge can help. Best, of course, to be there by the impeccable right of family inheritance. The whole object is to appear to belong, like moss on a stable roof.

Lower Middle Class

The fringe class to which the majority of the population of the British Isles belongs without admitting to do so. No-one will confess to it. It is something like having bad breath. Other people are more aware of it than you are. Moreover the plain fact of the matter is that most of us are in it.

Much of the time and effort of this class is simply devoted to trying to stay there and not fall even lower into the dreaded working-classes. The rest of their time is spent trying to graduate, by almost any means, into the Middle Middle (or, less hopefully, Upper Middle) Class strata. And all the time Lower Middle Class preserves are being remorselessly attacked by the growth of Lower Class affluence. It's tough in this position.

Status is only maintained by an hysterical and precarious adherence to standards of taste – precarious because they can change so rapidly. In fact, all material manifestations of class are more important to the upholders of the Lower Middle Class, than to any other group in society.

To maintain a Middle Class position, it is no longer sufficient to own a colour television or a washing-machine (though a washing-up-machine might still just suffice) or a Ford Sierra or to have holidays in Majorca. The Lower Classes now have these things as well. This forces Lower Middle Class families to spend far more than they can afford. Consequently, as a class, they are the hardest up of all.

The **Middle Class** see themselves as the upholders of decency, hard-work, and common-sense.

They see themselves as the 'bastions of Society.'

Upper Lower Class

There is no disadvantage today in belonging here. In fact, there are many advantages. From here you can enjoy all the privileges that money can buy (like getting into golf and Rotary clubs) without needing to subscribe to all the frantic snobbery that is essential to maintain Lower Middle Class status.

Upper Lower Class people who know where their place is and are not ashamed of it, are quite a privileged group. They include owners of businesses in such down-to-earth areas as the motor-car and building trades, and waste-disposal. They are also the commercially successful exponents of such traditionally Lower Class professions as Landladies and Bookies.

The Upper Lower Class world is one where taste and refinement are not only undesired but even scorned. They enjoy reading, watching, wearing, eating and drinking whatever they like.

Middle Lower Class

Surprisingly, statistics will show that the genuine lower classes (or what used to be called the 'Working-Class' before the Government established unemployment as an accepted vocation) have always accounted for quite a small percentage of the population – as little as 10 per cent. They are consequently a proud minority who enjoy such privileges as:

a) zealous union protection
b) public and private vulgarity
c) annoying the Middle Classes
d) wholehearted addiction to soccer and sex.

The Middle Lower Class are easily stirred into simulated protest, a sort of hangover from their peasant days. They are generally happy to be able to afford Middle Class comforts without the desire to benefit from them socially.

Lower Lower Class

The lowest of the low or, as known in India, the 'untouchables'. There is no need to be shy about saying this as they will not be offended. Indeed, they are inordinately proud of their position to which they got by making no effort at all.

The Lower Lowers are people who have long discarded all pretentions, hopes, or need to display class, in the generally accepted sense – though they have it on their own terms. You will find honest occupations such as dustman drawn, as a hereditary right, from this class; and other such jobs that no-one who considered himself Middle Lower Class or above would think of doing. The class also includes on a sort of transitory basis, students, the audiences that commercial television rounds up for quiz games and most professional footballers – in short, anyone who has either fallen out of society or has not yet contrived to climb into it.

The **Lower Class** see themselves as the good companions of life, comrades-in-arms, honest, upright, and hard-working.

They see themselves as 'the salt of the Earth'.

GENERAL OBSERVATIONS

To summarise the Class situation in broad terms, the following truisms should be accepted:

1. That it is just possible, by concentrated effort, to move up a class; but it is virtually impossible to go down. An impoverished Duke drawing the dole would still be Upper Class. That is the ineffable and immovable nature of the thing. This is, of course, reinforced by the obvious fact that very few people, beyond a few left-wing politicians and churchmen, ever actually want to go down.

2. Class is 95 per cent inherited but it can be adjusted by inter-breeding on the Mendelian principle. If an Upper Class parent married a Lower Class parent and they had three children; one would be Upper Class, one would be Lower Class and the other would be desperately unhappy.

3. Many do not particularly want to be the class they are. But you should never try to take a person's class away from them, even if you mean it in kindness. It can leave them with absolutely nothing by way of character.

4. There is no such thing as a classless society, not even in the animal world. Anybody who has kept rabbits or pigeons will know that they can be Upper, Middle and Lower Class like anyone else.

5. Everyone believes they are classless but they never fool anyone else.

6. Those who indulge in the constant battle for class promotion generally find that it is like rowing across an uphill stretch of water. They may come to the conclusion that it is an unscientific pursuit and, acquiring wisdom in old age, they very often give it up.

7. All foreigners are automatically a class lower than their equivalent in one's own country. Many backward countries which used to have only two classes, Upper and Lower Lower, have now developed their own class systems, and the essential Middle Classes have been carefully created and nurtured even in Communist societies.

8. In a survey in which people were asked what class they thought they belonged to, 10 per cent considered themselves Upper, 68 per cent believed they were Middle, 12 per cent conceded that they were Lower. The other 10 per cent were not sure. Observations bear out that the percentages were rather biased toward aggrandisement. The real assessment would be that 5 per cent are Upper, 50 per cent Middle, 45 per cent Lower – or thereabouts.

PRINCIPAL HATES

Upper Class: Believers in anything. Fuss. The Lower Class.
Middle Class: Buses. Unions. The Upper and the Lower Class.
Lower Class: The Upper Class. The police. Tolerance.

The Plight of the Middle Class

It will be noted throughout the ensuing pages that we are continually drawn to conclude that the Upper and Lower Classes have a great deal in common, quite apart from the fact that the one can go no higher and the other can go no lower. This certainly accounts for their shared unambiguous outlook. Beyond this they share such facets as irregularity of features, contorted speech, horse-racing, cruel sports, a liking for seafood (smoked salmon and jellied eels), and a united contempt for the Middle Class.

It is the middle Class who are mainly concerned with safeguarding and improving their lot, eternally tidal in the insecurity of their position. They would like to be thought higher and are terrified of being thought lower. They hover in their vulnerable middle position in a state of constant dissatisfaction. They suffer badly from qualms.

The Middle Class find the art of bluffing as necessary to their existence as the smell of saddle soap is to the Upper Class and the smell of frying to the Lower. Bluffing about Class is not merely a fringe activity like bluffing in Music or Golf (though bluffing in these areas is mainly to do with proving class) but an essential part of everyday life. Middle Class golfers know that it is much better to say, nonchalantly, that they belong to Wentworth than admit to using the public course at Worthing. On the other hand, living at Worthing is better than living in Wandsworth. And a holiday in the South of France is worth two in Stoke-on-Trent. All of which is based on the desire to give the impression that whatever you do has cost a lot of money which you can well afford. Of no other class can it be said so pointfully that living can damage your health.

CLASS-SPOTTING

It is clearly an enormous asset to be adept at class-spotting. The joy is that it can be done with a minimum of physical effort or bibliographical research: all you have to do is observe. It is particularly important, of course, to be able to detect the genuine article from the assumed or phoney one. Once you have established that someone is false it means that you can more readily establish your own shaky alibi. If he is real however, you must be much more careful, as he is in a strong position to call your bluff. The best position from which to bluff, as has been said in other contexts, is either honesty or complete duplicity. The halfway position is not a good idea.

What you must watch out for is the true trait coming out in spite of best endeavours and imposing its genuineness on the assumed mannerisms. For instance, a person may speak with a posh accent and even have a stiff upper lip or wear a deer-stalker, but the discerning bluffer will know that he or she is not the genuine article if the shoes are not made of leather. Once you can spot a deviation of this kind, you will be more able to:

a) pursue your own line of deceit; or
b) unmercifully, but slowly and carefully, destroy the facades of those who set out to deceive.

The main areas for class spotting are:

- Speech and associated Vocabulary
- Names
- Manners
- Taste
- Faces
- Clothes

Speech

Once upon a time the most obvious distinguishing
mark of the Upper echelons of society was the way
they spoke. In Shakespeare's times all the Upper Class
spoke in grandiose blank verse and used words like
'multitudinous', and sounded like Sir John Gielgud.
The Middle Class, a rare breed then, dropped into a
quaint sort of 'verily thou hast' but generally un-
poetical mode. The Lower Class dropped all pretences to verse and indulged in witless saws in a sort of
Dorset accent – 'th'art a pig's bladder full o' flat ale', etc.

In more recent times, the well-bred affected what
was called The Oxford Accent. Looked on as a deroga-
tory adjunct, it was rather unfair on Oxford to be thus
associated as those who used it had acquired it long
before they were connected with that hallowed shrine
of education and motor cars. Nevertheless a fair
proportion of those who got to Oxford did have the
vocal characteristics which were largely acquired on a
hereditary basis or at various expensive schools and
should more accurately have been identified as the
Public School Accent. It was, and is, used with equal
identification and effect by those whose mental equipment did not take them to University – Army officers
and the like. Those who wish to acquire it as a bluffing
aid will have to practise before a mirror as it is largely
achieved through facial distortion. For instance, 'I say,
old boy!' should be said with a twist of the right hand
side of the upper lip of the kind that would be essential
if you were trying to keep a monocle in position.

The educated Middle Classes, not wishing to sound
like characters in a Noel Coward play, adopted what
was called the King's English; a rather confusing term
as most Kings were of foreign extraction. It was the

public school accent with most of the exaggerated vowel sounds tuned down. The object then was to conceal your origins as if there was something rather disgraceful about being born in Devon or Yorkshire. Thus in the early days of broadcasting, BBC announcers spoke in language and tones of such purity, dressed in dinner jackets even when unseen, that all connections with the human race, let alone a county, were successfully concealed.

The sudden change in recent years to common speech must be credited to television which has revealed to those who live in the civilised world that there is life in Liverpool and Birmingham which can be successfully maintained without a total grasp of English.

No longer does the House of Commons speak with the accents of Eton and Oxford. Many of them sound as if they had never been to school at all. Today, if you wish to be heard publicly it can actually be a positive disadvantage not to have a regional accent or at least something odd about your speech, *especially* in broadcasting.

Having a country accent has never been a drawback to the Lower Class, indeed it gives them a bit of an edge. But having a city accent, e.g. Manchester or Glasgow, is simply to emphasise Lower Class origins. The Lower Class speaker uses the speech pattern that happens to be around him, whether it be Cockney or Llandudno Welsh, Cornish burr or Lincolnshire bauble. The true son of Birmingham unashamedly speaks Brummagem – at least until he hears himself recorded.

An accent is particularly detectable on the telephone for some reason. Once you have discovered some such twang you may proceed to look for other small flaws in the general disguise.

Vocabulary

This is now a much surer guide to Class than accent. Generally speaking it is high-class to call a spade a spade or, in more practical everyday terms (for very few people actually talk about spades), a lavatory a lavatory. It is Upper Class not to say anything about it at all but just go. The Middle Class are the ones who tend to mutter something about the desire 'to spend a penny'.

Upper Class people have a very small vocabulary. Their public utterances are noteworthy for their avoidance of actually saying anything that commits them to a clear line of thought or opinion (a model that has been successfully copied by many top politicians and prominent churchmen). Upper Class views on almost anything have long been encapsulated into the phrase 'a damn good show' or conversely, 'a damn bad show'. Indeed *everything* is either good or bad, the two words usually sufficing to cover their entire emotional gamut of opinion; though occasionally the word 'shambles' is uttered to describe something beyond comprehension or about which a clear-cut decision has proved impossible. Upper Class vocabulary has remained remarkably archaic, there being no necessity for change. Ever economical of utterance, they maintain throughout their lives the childish delight in contractional familiarisation – as in 'champers' and 'preggers'.

A fine ear for distinctions is one of the assets of the Middle Class and it is a weapon that the bluffer would do well to master. For example, Middle Class words for man include 'chap' (borrowed from the Upper Class), 'bloke' and 'geezer' (borrowed from the Lower Class), 'guy' (borrowed from the USA) and 'character' (one of their own). Their usage is constantly varied by qualifying adjectives, such as 'nice chap', 'queer bloke', 'funny old geezer', 'weird character', which helps to establish the correct assignation. One would not say 'good geezer' or 'funny old guy' for instance. Women (again in imitation of Upper Class gallantry) are referred to collectively as 'the girls', regardless of age. The other outstanding Middle Class vocabularistic tendency is the latching on to 'current' words, a subsconscious demonstration of having read the right papers. These include words like 'viable' (meaning it might work) and 'legendary' (meaning anyone who has done anything, however small, to make their name a household one) – particularly used in entertainment and sport – 'the legendary Zubelik' (i.e. a runner from Eastern Europe whom the commentator heard about last week).

Lower Class vocabulary is, as one would expect, also of refined simplicity. Their word for man is 'bloke' and women are only referred to in an indirect sort of way as 'her' or 'she'. A Lower Class male addresses another one as 'mate', sometimes 'Jim' (or in Scotland 'Jimmy') – a form of address lately taken up by the Middle Class in a jocular sort of way.

Importance must be attached not so much to how you address others as how you are addressed. A constant effort must be made to appear on top, as it were. The object is to go into a shop or garage and be addressed as 'sir' or 'madam'. If the chap behind the counter (this particularly applies to newsagents who, in serving all classes, become great levellers) refers to a middle-class gentleman as 'mate' or 'young feller' (jokingly) all pretensions are punctured for at least two days. Any woman who goes into a shop and is asked, 'What would you like, dearie' should immediately attend to her image until she has regained full 'What-can-I-do-for-you,-Madam' status.

Names

If you took any notice of Shakespeare and comic writers like P. G. Wodehouse, you would think that the Upper Class tend to go for a small range of fanciful names such as Algernon, Percival, Marmaduke, Montmorency, Agatha and Felicity. In fact, they show a marked preference for ordinary Middle Class names like Charles, David and Mary. The Royal Family are a good example of this. It doesn't matter too much, anyway, as Uppers delight in calling each other by such familiar endearments as Boo-Boo, Babs and Tigger.

The Middle Class like to give their children names which they fondly imagine have quality; but they frequently misfire with things like Pelham, Dornford and Florence which no Upper Class child would be seen dead with. Or else they go for the safe ones like John, Peter, May and Kathleen. There are some basically Middle Class names, however, that could not belong elsewhere, like Bryan, Geoffrey, Herbert, Stanley, Ronald, Margery, Prudence and Clare.

The Lower Class don't believe that people should really have names at all and much prefer to call everyone 'mate' or 'luv'. When they have to face up to the embarrassment of an appellation, they like it to be as short as possible, and the ones they use are frequently abbreviations of some of the above – Fred, Joe, Sid, Bill, Alf, Jim, Marge, Flo, and Eth.

Acute bluffers will point out immediately that it doesn't always work. There have been, for example, very important Harolds – two adjacent Prime Ministers of totally different classes were both Harolds. It could be that the Upper Class one in this instance was mistakenly named.

So names are one of the class things that you have to be able to see through right away. If someone says to you: 'Hello, I'm George', it could quite well be the King of England. Unlikely, but it could have been. The prefix King can do wonders for a name. Always in the full form, of course – King Frederick or King William is all right, but King Fred or King Bill would not do at all.

You should be particularly wary of the Middle Class male who tends to favour Lower Class abbreviations, particularly for use in all-male or sporting clubs. Here Fred can actually sound quite classy. There are some shorties that are essentially Middle class like Tom, Les, Chris and Ron. Occasionally the Middle Classes will jovialise a name, e.g. Johnny for John and Willie for Bill.

If introduced to someone called Herbert, William, Alfred or Lionel you should start calling him Herb, Bill, Alf or Li as soon as possible. It can cut them down a whole class in one syllable.

Manners

It is a somewhat old-fashioned, but staunchly surviving, view that manners are indicative of class. In some sections of the community they have been relinquished altogether but this is mainly in areas of public and private service – banks, shops, transport, and local government departments. Manners, though less prominent than they were, are still a part of the social and domestic scene.

The Upper Class have never been aware of any problems in this area. They simply behave naturally and rely on their hereditary sense of rightness. The instilling of manners in their offspring is greatly aided by the fact that these are strictly brought up by retainers while they are at the biddable stage and trained like gun-dogs. Amongst themselves the Upper Class are boisterously rude, referring to their crude behaviour as 'high spirits', but they approach anyone of a lower class with studied politeness and have earned quite a good reputation in this respect.

The Lower Class have no manners in the accepted sense and thus identify themselves. They see them as an artifical imposition on normal behaviour and therefore pretentious and dishonest. But they still admonish their young with such phrases as 'Mind your manners, now, young Fred' as an undemanding concession to Middle Class morality.

It is the Middle Class who observe the Victorian rules of etiquette – not drinking out of the saucer, the correct holding of knives and forks, wearing the right colour of shoes, having and using a handkerchief. They like to be thought of as well-behaved and only dispense with manners, as do others, when driving a car.

Taste

Taste is entirely a Middle Class concern. The Lower Class don't have it and the Upper Class don't need it. While surrounding oneself with tasteful things is made easier by having a well-filled wallet, spending power does not necessarily confer taste. The difficulty here is that taste is fluctuating and personalised, and greatly depends on what Sunday paper you read. Even one's best friends can lack taste and fill their houses with things that you wouldn't even give as presents. Social bluffing is an endless succession of slight shudders and veiled hints. It is not done to say 'Why on earth did you paint your windows yellow?' What you say is "We always think that white sets off things so well", in such a way that any defence of yellow is unthinkable.

While there are no absolute criteria in these matters, there are some generally accepted mores of bad and good taste that are considered reliable indicators of class:

Examples of Bad Taste
— Garden gnomes
— Clothes with slogans written on them
— Paintings by Landseer
— Wall ducks
— Things hanging in or stuck on the windows of cars
— The wearing of tennis pumps with evening dress
— Keeping ferrets
— *The Benny Hill Show*
— Tchaikovsky

It should be noted, however, that such items are often displayed by people of taste as an elaborate sort of joke. If the joke falls flat then they can always say 'Yes isn't it awful but it was given to us by (an aunt, the children, some friends, etc.)'.

Examples of Good Taste
— Home-grown vegetables
— Anything white (provided it is clean)
— Water-colours
— Staffordshire pottery (however hideous)
— Large dogs (however hairy and smelly)
— Siamese cats
— *Yes Minister*
— Elgar
— Us

Faces

It is not easy to specify class characteristics in the face. Some of the things seen there are the result of other traits that are nothing to do with class, e.g. sexuality, intellect, insanity, avariciousness and alcohol, and all classes can be equally afflicted by such things.

Nevertheless there are certain conglomerate aspects of the face, which do reflect class and breeding. They are most positive in the Upper and Lower Classes as the Middles have affiliations with foreigners and, in general, are less insular in their outlook.

The most prominent feature of an Upper Class face is probably the mouth. The line of the upper lip is often mis-shapen as a result of the vowels that pass through it. Upper Class features tend to be irregular in most aspects, the eyes not at the same height, the nose veering to one side, the older face deeply lined. The overall effect is precisely what you might expect – a sort of nobility – like a moose that has seen better days.

The Lower Class face is almost the opposite of this. Although it too becomes very wrinkled in advanced old age it tends to keep a bland robustness into advanced middle-age at least. The lack of concern with intellectual matters and an untroubled conscience clearly help to achieve this. Lower Class young tend to be handsome and sexy in appearance. They have straight mouths and good teeth to match the general excellence of their bodies.

The Middle Class face is more inhibited, more calculated in effect. Most Middle Class people are obsessively living up to something or trying to impress. Their faces therefore take on a more conscious pose. Anyone wearing a look of displeasure, disdain, disbelief, disgust, disassociation or any other disses you care to mention, is almost certainly Middle Class. The men have a greater tendency toward moustaches and beards which are used to disguise the dramatic failure of their faces. The women achieve a similar effect with make-up and hair. If a face strikes you as being in conflict with the inner soul, it is almost certainly a Middle Class face.

Clothes

The student of bluffing will soon come to realise that clothes are one of the most reliable class identifications of all. Like feathers on birds. The point about clothes is that they are adopted by the wearer (whether consciously or not) to make a certain desired impression.

The Upper Class go for the 'haven't two pennies to rub together' look. (e.g. Lord Longford) which has the advantage that if it happens to be true nobody notices the difference. Their clothing tends to be made of tough tweedy material that ensures a long life, not for economical reasons but because it has to withstand the abrasive effects of being jumped at by large numbers of dogs, passing through gorse and heather in search of wild life to be shot at, rubbing against horses and sitting on madly uncomfortable furniture.

For similar considerations both sexes tend to wear what are described as 'sensible' shoes, things like brogues, always laced-up and leather soled. A pair of Upper Class travellers were recently spotted in the Underground near Hammersmith, a rare phenomenon only explained by the fact that it was a Heathrow train. The female of the species was correctly dressed in a very hairy bullet-proof outfit with an outspoken rather than loud check pattern, a jumper and pearls. She also sported a cloak of the same material, a sort of sawn-off shepherd's crook and a genuine Gladstone bag (now very scarce and valuable). Her brogues had protruding tongues such as are now generally found on golfing shoes. Perhaps they *were* golfing shoes, which she had absent-mindedly kept on. The man wore a tweedy trilby with a minute rim and a game-bird feather, a shirt with a very narrow collar and an unidentified club tie. The rest of him apart from narrowly cut tweedy trousers was hidden under the orthodox dirty, heavy-duty mackintosh. His shoes looked as if they were worth every bit of £300 and he carried a thick walking-stick and a hold-all that was clearly a family heirloom. They sat in the tube-train, the focus of attention amongst the more familiar jeans and saris of regular tube-travellers. They spoke in their normal loud neighing tones, apparently under the impression that they were still in their own drawing-room. A superb pair of specimens possibly caught on a migratory flight. There was no doubt that they were genuinely Upper Class rather than Middle Class phoneys for they had the genuine grouse-moor complexions not normally seen in the City, and when an inspector got on and found they had no tickets it was he who did the apologising for having bothered them.

For general indoor wear Upper Class men still favour a rather drab pin-striped sort of 'demob' suit so unendearingly cut that it looks organic. On formal occasions they wear dinner jackets whose lapels are turning green with age, while the ladies (including those of the Royal Family) appear to have access to strangely out-dated garments that most people would not easily come by. Fabrics and tiaras that, on Middle Class women, would give the impression of the wearer being on the way to a fancy-dress ball, take on an air of well-bred normality. That is real class.

One may also detect a true Upper Class wearer by looking, as it were, beneath the surface. It is a case of a body made to fit a horse being clothed in garments made to fit a man. Look for bowing of the legs and elongation of the buttocks. Another give-away is that Upper Class trousers stop short of the ankle; giving an impression of having shrunk in the rain or that the wearer has unexpectedly grown in the night.

The Middle Class are in their usual quandary when it comes to clothes. They are torn between the urge to be shabby in an Upper Class way or smart in the way that fashion magazines tell them they ought to be. Emulating their betters the men will buy tailor-made suits but ones that are made by tailors who only know how to make 'off the peg' garments. Whichever side they dress, as they say in the trade, the tailor usually seems to have got it wrong. The Lower Middle Class man, epitomised by the junior executive, is acutely aware of what he is wearing. Continuously on the watch for changes in fashion he generally finds that they change so quickly that he has only just bought a pair of tight trousers when flares suddenly come in. He always shows a lavish amount of cuff which has to be hitched up periodically to expose his expensive gadget-covered watch.

The Middle Classes get in a special tangle over jeans. Not able to go so far as to adopt the skin-tight poured-in look of the Lower Classes, Middle Class breeding makes Middle Class men or women lose their nerve at some point. Anyone seen in jeans that are definitely baggy and totally unenhancing may be taken, with 99 per cent certainty, to be Middle Class.

Lower Class wear is quite simply anything that is tasteless, obnoxious or ludicrous in Middle Class eyes, e.g. floral short-sleeved shirts open to the waist and revealing a beer-paunch; black nylon dresses, plastic shoes; 'kiss me quick' hats, and dangly earrings in the daytime. Only when being defiantly Lower Class, or in soap operas, do Lower Class ladies wear knotted scarves round their heads and hair-curlers.

Hats and Caps

Special consideration must be given to caps (especially cloth caps) and hats.

Cloth caps might seem a truly ambiguous class symbol, being associated in common language usage with Working Class guise; yet, through their sporting associations, they are also a frequent item of Upper Class wear. Seen side by side, the differences, however, are quite apparent. The Working Class cap is much floppier than the Upper Class one. It is made of a cheaper, less rigid material so that its upper part looks something like an empty hot-water bottle. It is usually patterned with a small anonymous check and has a largish peak. It is always slightly dirty or at least it should look well-worn, as it is a considerable embarrassment to a Working Class man to appear in a brand new cap. He will therefore make some attempt to break it in before appearing in public in it, secretly wearing it in the pigeon-loft, in bed or while underneath the family car. Rural workers have especially dirty caps that smell of organic matter and are of indeterminate colour. This is the true traditional cap that was touched, or doffed, in the presence of a person of superior class.

The Upper Class cap, as worn for clay-pigeon

shooting or point-to-point races is much smaller and fairly rigid, being made of first-class material such as Harris tweed or cavalry twill. It has a very short peak, and in profile it looks like a slice of cheese. It has to be tighter fitting, of course, so that it won't fall off in the more active moments of sport. It rarely has to be removed unless royalty are present.

The Middle Class wear hats, not caps. The favourite used to be the trilby made of felt with a silk band round it and a silk or leather lining inside, which would get very seedy and greasy. Occasionally, to give a sporting aspect, a small feather would be stuck into the band. There was always a dint in the middle unless the owner was agricultural or eccentric. In that case it might be worn without a dint which had the result of making the rim go floppy. The Class-Spotter can almost cry when he considers the demise of the bowler, once the distinguishing mark of the Middle Class business man. And the topper which signified that its owner was either Upper Middle or Lower Upper Class or else an undertaker. Even undertakers have now gone off them.

The average man no longer wears a hat of any kind. He discovered how much it reveals his class.

MAIN PASSIONS

Upper Class: Horses (jumping, racing, breeding, etc.). Large, hairy dogs. Shooting (now known as conservation).

Middle Class: None (they have likes and dislikes but are not passionate about anything).

Lower Class: Horses (betting on). Soccer.

CLASS SYMBOLS

Cars

If you didn't have your own carriage you either took the next stagecoach or walked. This was the situation when the car first came in and was purchased by the monied Upper Class and one or two dukes. The names these vehicles bore reflected their Upper Class intent. Rolls-Royce though not actually a double-barrelled name but the partnership of two, gave the right impression. The cloth caps of the gentry were seen whizzing by in gleaming monsters imperiously blowing large brass bulb-horns. The Middle Class and the Lower Class either got out of the way or got killed. No questions were asked. A famous cartoon went as follows: Upper Class Driver: 'We must be getting near a town!' Upper Class Passenger: 'Why do you say that?' Upper Class Driver: 'We are running over more people.'

It was not long before brash Americans like Ransom E. Olds and Henry Ford came along and started to build cars in which the Middle Class and the Lower Class could now be seen also dashing about everywhere looking for members of the Upper Class to run over. It is regrettable to have to say it, but money became almost as important as class in the future selection of cars. In fact many cars, like Rolls-Royces, Bentleys, Aston Martins, etc., had to be sold at inflated prices just to keep them in the hands of the right people. This inbuilt safety measure still works to some extent and people still expect an Upper Class figure to get out of one of these machines. They are often disappointed when a Lower Class film star or a scrap-metal merchant emerges (you can tell the latter by their hairy arms).

Class ploys now available to the public are limited. The mere ownership of a Rover or a Jaguar is not sufficient since these are frequently to be found outside council houses. All that is available is a temporary ploy (sometimes of only a week or so's duration) like being the first to have a car with this year's registration number or a Mini with tinted glass.

The bluffer, in conversation, will have to cope quite regularly with THE CAR used as a class symbol. Obviously there is little that can be done about the person who says (with inevitable casualness) 'I run a Rolls' (or Bentley). Possession of one of these might almost confer the status of Upper Class on anyone; at least, while they're in it.

There follows a simple guide to car classes.

Upper Class Cars
- All vintage cars. These are not all owned by the Upper Class but they undoubtedly elevate their owners. An intimate knowledge of their innards is essential, even by those who have no other artisan leanings.
- Rolls-Royce/Bentley/Daimler
- Rovers prior to 1960 – the ones that look like tanks with big sides and small windows. Also green and muddy Range Rovers.
- Morris Minors – the classless car, equally at home on the country or the council estate.

Middle Class Cars
- Volvos, Hondas, Renaults, Ford Granadas and Sierras. The Upper, Middle and Lower Middle Class grading is largely imposed by the makers in

their brochures. The larger, more expensive models are usually photographed in the Highlands with dogs looking out of the window. The smaller ones are generally pictured as being full of bright young things with surf boards.

Lower Class Cars

- Old models of almost any of the above. The Lower Class believe in running their cars into the ground as a matter of principle, rather than economic necessity.
- Large tinny cars like Ford Zodiacs and Chryslers, of garish (generally multi) colouring and with big tyres. The most sought after are those which emit a lot of smoke from their exhausts to cause maximum irritation to the occupants of Upper and Middle Class cars.
- Minis. Particularly liked by Lower Class youth, but driven by many Middle Class eccentrics in a spirit of inverted snobbery.
- 3–wheeled cars, other than invalid models.
- Large American cars with loose bumpers.

Habitat

There is little need to detail the life style of the genuine Upper Upper Class family. For the price of a ticket you can wander round their crumbling castles and estates (except during the breeding season) and marvel at the conditions of discomfort under which the Upper Class live.

You may examine every room (except the W.C.) and wonder how anyone could possibly sit on such ill-designed chairs and live with such gloomy paintings.

The rugs, although worn, are obviously expensive but inclined to slide on the highly polished floors.

There are not enough castles for the Middle Upper Class (except in Scotland where there are too many) so they tend to live in mansions that have more accomodation than they really need or can maintain, or in very large flats near Regent's park with huge rooms like those you see in films that stretch as far as the eye can see. The dominating features are large sofas covered in chintz. They are covered in chintz because they are falling to pieces underneath; moth has got at the original fabric, and woodworm at the frame. To be properly Lower Upper Class or Upper Middle Class you must live in a large house with a mimimum of central heating, and chintz should dominate.

The Middle Middle Class often live in houses that are, or resemble, decaying vicarages. They are distinguished by the possession of heirlooms, not a plethora of them like the Upper Class have, but isolated, highly polished pieces of furniture that they refuse to sell, silver salvers and over-large pieces of china. The Middle Middle Class pay great attention to carpets which are always of good quality. Even when they have to move from their large house to a smaller one in retirement they take all these things with them now displayed in closer, even cramped, proximity. You have to be careful not to walk into the grandfather clock believing it to be the way out.

With the Lower Middle Class we come to one of the classes who actually buy and live among new objects (including heirlooms purchased in antique shops). In fact, most of their new things may well have been carefully selected to look old and high class. They are quite happy with period imitations including prints of local landmarks and brass ships' barometers. The

Lower Middle Class home is simply an extension of their struggle for class promotion. It is usually bursting with video and electronic equipment and those curiously widely bought but unreadable books by authors like le Carré.

Upper Lower Class people are the ones who buy anything that is not-quite-nice. If they see something going cheaply they buy it, or if they see something cheap at a high price they buy it. It is they who have the obligatory row of Peter Scott ducks winging across the wall, and all their furniture is varnished. They spend a lot of money on cushions, carpets, curtains, that never seem to match.

The true Lower Class are sitting on a gold-mine. Their possessions, done up a bit, would be eagerly snapped up by the Middle Class in antique shops. Even the milk-jug with 'A Present from Southend' written on it.

Pets

The association of man with the rest of the animal kingdom is of paramount importance in the defining of class structures. Basically the only pets that matter, in this respect, are dogs and horses.

Dogs are straightforward. They have well-defined class strata of their own. Obviously they can't help it if they are taken into a family that is beneath them but you can always tell by the look on their faces. To start with, big dogs tend to be Upper Class simply because they like to roam round estates; Great Danes and Borzois are not really built for semi-detached existences. Some people do keep St. Bernards in smallish houses for a short time, but they tend to lose their friends. Gun-dogs of various kinds are Upper

Class dogs but actually only the Pointer (strangely, because it has always been considered rude to point) has maintained its status.

It is rather sad to have to mention Labradors at all. The truth is that labradors are ornamental gun-dogs, and have been taken up by the Middle Classes who would dearly like to project a hint of some loose connection with the gun-toting Upper Class. Labradors generally fail, however, to add the required sporty touch because most of them, living in Middle Class opulence, are too fat to run, can't swim, have no sense of direction, and are amiable cowards. They have become what Thurber classifies as 'Lawn-dogs'.

Setters and Spaniels have become very popular with the Middle Classes. Corgis, as everyone knows, are very high-class. And any dog that can be considered a hound (though it should not be called a hound-dog) is pretty well placed be it fox, basset, blood or just plain Beagle. Being country dogs gives them status. The only exception is the Greyhound which has become a working class dog (reduced to running after a stuffed hare) and the Whippet, which always was.

Some breeds have definitely come down in the world through over-use as status symbols. It is no good, for instance, anybody thinking that having a Poodle cuts any ice. French or not, they are still likely to find themselves with quite Lower Class owners and living in the sort of houses where people also have tropical fish. Terriers are variable; rough-haired ones, including the Scottish variety, are still highly rated, but smooth-haired ones, particularly the Jack Russell, are definitely not. The Bull-dog is a fairly classless dog but the Pug is high. The Pekingese is very Middle Class but can be seen in Upper Middle Class and Lower Upper Class homes. The mongrel, it goes without saying, is thoroughly Lower Class but it can be found elsewhere either by mistake or because the gate was left open.

Horses are tremendously important in the class struggle. They were established at an early stage as bestowing class status and this still applies. There is no better way of acquiring a higher class than having, or simply riding, horses. To possess one (even if it is kept in somebody else's field) is definitely an asset. It implies the essential possession of stables, paddocks, lots of people to look after them and the flair for wearing riding gear. Upper Class horses tend to be very big, the higher the better so that the rider can tower above his rivals. Military horses are also big and it is interesting to note that because of this cavalry regiments tend to think themselves a cut above others, even though they now usually drive tanks. It is not altogether infra dig to ride a small horse. Those that do avoid saying 'I have a small horse' by saying 'I have a pony'.

'Pony' has, in fact, become quite an Upper Class word because there are pony clubs (nobody seems to join horse clubs – not even horses) and because of polo-ponies. This makes them very high class. Shetland ponies are simply ponies whose legs haven't grown properly, and they are only ridden by small children with the same affliction.

It is unarguably Upper Class to possess even a small herd of Highland cattle or deer and, in the bird world, coveys of pheasants, partridges or grouse. Farm animals, on the whole, do not greatly affect class; Upper, Middle or Lower may equally have rights to considerable droves of cows and gain nothing from it one way or the other. Pigs, likewise, although they are generally considered to be Low Class animals, because of their habits and their associations with sausages, can cut across the class structure.

Cats are much less effective as class symbols because they live a life that is independent of their owners. They don't take up much room and are happy to sleep on window-ledges, etc. where no-one else wants to be. The majority of cats are of uncertain breed, and ordinary tabbies and black cats are likely to be found in any class of house. Even the long haired ones, like Persians, although they try to look Upper Class, are at home anywhere.

Most cage birds are basically Lower Class (or at best Lower Middle Class), especially budgerigars, canaries and pigeons (though fantails tastefully arrayed around a dovecote can confer higher status). The possession of peacocks is, on the other hand, Upper Class, because you generally have to have the background and space to set them off properly.

The tortoise is uniquely classless because it has nothing to offer and is virtually non-existent for most of its life. Most reptiles are only possessed, like single sheep, by eccentric persons. Zoo animals, though there are exceptions, hardly come under the category of pets. They are only kept in large numbers by the Upper Class and Laurence Durrell.

PARTICULAR PLEASURES

Upper Class: House-parties. Hunting. Drinking. Breeding.

Middle Class: Golfing. Going for a spin. Eating. Childless sex. Wine.

Lower Class: Drinking beer in overcrowded pubs. Watching television. Breeding.

CLASS AFFILIATIONS

Class warfare is not simply, as you may think, the bitter battle that goes on between the Upper Class Establishment (supported by the Middle Class who are bribed into co-operation by the bestowal of honours twice a year) against the Lower Class banded together in Unions. That is a comparatively harmless business and usefully keeps people's minds off foreign affairs. Far more serious class warfare is going on all around us. In territorial movements, for instance. As fast as the Middle Class manage to occupy a street in Islington and have a Lower Class terrace tarted up, the Lower Class will manage to infiltrate into Shepherds Bush and, in no time at all, have turned a row of elegant Victorian houses into derelict shells and filled them with West Indians. The classes are perpetually at war in these kinds of spontaneous skirmishes.

Marriage

As everyone knows, marriage is rife with class complications. The first matter that is discussed (certainly in Middle Class circles and upwards) when two people get engaged is whether one or the other is marrying beneath them. In fact, because females consider themselves to be one class above the male, it is inevitably the woman who is marrying beneath her.

Lower Class people tend to get married at an early age and often in a hurry. The Upper Class also get married young, hustled into it by families eager that offspring be provided to keep the breed going. The

Middle Class, on the whole, get married in less of a rush but even then frequently manage to get married to the wrong person. They prefer their offspring not to marry into the Lower Class, but they frequently do, thus producing the Lower Middle and Upper Lower brackets.

For some reason marriage brings out the worst kind of snobbery with remarks like 'His father used to work in the Post Office you know', 'Just because he went to Oxford', 'I never thought she would marry a dentist' – and so on. Except in the very Upper Class, where there is little option if the estate is to be kept intact, people rarely marry someone who is of exactly the same class and they will constantly remind each other of this one way or another. Otherwise, marriage carries no mark of social distinction – possibly even the opposite.

Divorce, on the other hand, adds considerably to a person's rank in life. People who have been divorced several times can actually move into quite elevated circles.

Politics

British politics are entirely based on class. Earnest pretences are made to try to convince the voters that other considerations are involved but this doesn't deceive anyone.

Basically Conservatives are Upper Class, Liberals are Middle Class and Socialists are Lower Class. The simplicity and rightness of this arrangement is, however, complicated by many things.

To begin with, the converse statements are not true; all Upper Classes are not Conservative, all Middle Classes are not Liberal, otherwise we would always have a Liberal government; and all Lower Classes are not Socialists. This does not invalidate the earlier statement. The confusion arises from the fact that everyone is aiming to be a class higher. People vote Conservative not because they actually believe that anything is worth conserving (apart from the class system) but because it gives them an air of respectability and may confuse others as to their true origins.

For example, it will be found that 99 per cent of the kind of people who join Rotary Clubs or Women's Institutes will automatically vote Conservative. This, however remotely, gives them a link with the landed gentry and the Upper Class in general, even though they may actually be ideal material for the National Front and completely lacking in morals.

If the Upper Class alone voted Conservative there would be no Conservative governments since there are not enough of them. The Middle Class votes that the Conservatives get ought by rights to go to the Liberals who represent Middle Class views exactly in that they have no real policy or any overwhelming beliefs beyond a vague loyalty to the notion that the intellectual is superior to the worker, and that ties should still be worn. The Middle Class have been greatly discouraged from being themselves by the country's carefully contrived two-party system that has squeezed out a middle party, and by the lack of intelligent parliamentary candidates. An equally large proportion of the Middle Class vote Conservative simply because they do not like the Lower Class. They don't like the Upper Class either, but they dislike them less than they dislike the Lower Class.

As the Lower Class is larger in numbers than the Upper Class this should mean permanent Socialist governments, but it is prevented by a considerable number of the Lower Class also voting Conservative on the same grounds of respectability and possible elevation of class that make the Middle Class do it.

Lower Class voters predominantly vote Socialist not only because their fathers and grandfathers voted Socialist, but also because they hope that a Socialist government will abolish the Upper Class, and most of the Middle Class, so that they can themselves become the Upper Class. This never happens because most of the Socialist politicians are Middle Class Liberals and a few are even Upper Class. The Socialists tried to dispel this image by calling themselves the Labour Party, a ploy which never fooled anybody.

There are also other parties of an eccentric nature like the Communists and the Scottish Nationals, but as membership of these implies a belief in what you are voting for, they can never muster much of a following from any class.

British politics also includes the House of Lords which acts as a slight hindrance to the House of Commons' attempts to govern, but whose proper function is scarcely understood by anyone, least of all those who are in it. As they are all Lords or Ladies of some kind, a few of them actually Upper Class landed gentry, they should all theoretically be Upper Class and Conservative. Ultimately, if only from the mental confusion that results from continually being called a Lord, that is what they all gradually become; even those who were put there by the Socialists.

In the light of all this confusion it is not surprising that the two sides of British politics tend to be hopelessly well-balanced and little decisive progress is ever achieved. The last person to try to do anything positive was Oliver Cromwell and he was eventually defeated by the class system.

Occupations

The Upper Upper Class are mainly concerned with looking after their estates and controlling their tenants. Their main money-raising activity is agricultural – farming, forestry and the culling of species. Apart from this they might get involved in Middle Class charities. They get paid by the day for attending the House of Lords. The rest of the Upper Class are engaged in occupations that allow them to control other people's destinies, e.g. leading them into battle, sending them to prison, making new laws, raising bank and interest rates. They are usually directors of something.

The Middle Class are those who, under Upper Class or Upper Middle Class guidance, do any job which does not involve manual skills or which make the individual a paid entertainer.

The Lower Classes do things with their hands.

Directors

Everybody knows that the term 'Company Director' might mean anything from running an ice-cream cart to the I.C.I. – nonetheless it never seems to fail to impress. It can be used by all classes. Once you are a company director even if it is of a small under-capitalised publishing company in Tunbridge Wells, you are immediately written to by business management organisations, insurance companies and the American Express. Although company executive does not carry quite the same weight as company director, it can tip the scales slightly in the so designated's favour. It has a nice ambiguity about it: 'an executive of British Rail' (for example) might be anything from the Chairman to Fred at Halliford Halt who is everything from station master to wheel-tapper. It simply denotes a position which carries a degree of authority over someone else, combined with a minimal influence on policy making.

If directorship and executive status are combined, as in the term 'Managing Director', the weight carried is undeniable. But you have to have a fair number of people to push around before you can adopt such a title with confidence. You hardly ever hear of anyone being the Managing Director of a fish-and-chip shop.

The title 'Senior Executive' may only indicate senility but it does carry respect. The most rapacious class struggle and unease is apparent, however, in the ranks of the junior executives. Such a man might well come from Upper Class or Upper Middle Class ranks (in which case it is known as 'starting on the bottom rung'). His dogsbody position makes him feel decidedly Lower Middle Class, although he inwardly and devoutly believes himself worthy of higher status.

Junior executives (sometimes confusable with salesmen) nearly always drive in their shirt-sleeves, the only people who regularly use the little coat hooks provided in the rear. In their cars, company cars naturally of the Sierra or Cavalier range, they drive hard and dangerously and very close to the car in front, trying to give the impression that they are handling some impulsive machine like an Aston Martin and that they are on their way to clinch an important business deal that is vital to the country. They are quite simply terrified of being late again. Senior executives don't hurry. Managing Directors are chauffeur driven.

NB: Legal and medical people do not refer to themselves as directors or executives but as partners. Vets and dentists try to do the same without much success.

The Arts

The Arts have a curious position in the class-ridden society. The Arts started out by being unashamedly Lower Class or (at the most) Lower Middle Class. Everyone knows that musicians were once considered the lowest of the low. There were even laws passed to clarify this point. They have only just got past the 'tradesman's entrance' part of their history and even now they are discouraged from mingling with the guests. It is obligatory for pop musicians to be of Lower Class origins.

Artists are notoriously scruffy, smoke whatever is cheapest and drink bottled brown ale. Authors are the lowest common denominator in a generally low area of activity loosely known to the police as 'literature'. As for actors, 'actor' is simply a synonym for rogue and vagabond despite the efforts of the odd Upper Middle Class family to make it respectable. All the great writers, composers and artists worth mentioning were of Lower Class or, occasionally, Lower Middle Class origins; while the ancestry of many actors is untraceable as they were born in props-baskets during the pantomime season in Leeds. And yet many of them have ended up with knighthoods. However, it is generally understood that artistic knighthoods are not really social honours but simply a token gesture to the trade and all those who have suffered privation in the cause of Art.

One of the troubles of the artistic professions is that they do so little to help themselves. Rather than boosting the lot of their own kind they are always running them down and calling them charlatans. If, for example, Tchaikovsky states publicly that Brahms was a 'giftless bastard', who are the public, who know nothing of music, to contradict him.

The Upper Class has never really pretended that it liked or admired the Arts though they have frequently felt unable to avoid some degree of patronage. They dislike all artists except Landseer, all music except *Land of Hope and Glory* and they rarely read any author except Burke; the peerage, not the political thinker. Occasionally an Upper Class person has contributed to the Arts but generally as a letter-writer or a don.

The position of the Lower Class is very similar. They dislike all art except strip cartoons, all music except *Land of Hope and Glory* (unless still teen-age pop addicts) and they only read the sporting page of the *Sun* or the *Daily Mirror* except for the Conservative ones who read the *Daily Express*.

The Middle Class are the ones who entirely support the arts because:

a) they were taught to do so at school,
b) they mistakenly believe that it adds to their class status,
c) they actually like doing so.

Their favourite Middle class composer is Tchaikovsky (with Paul McCartney a close second); their favourite author Dickens (though they never actually read him); and their favourite artist Picasso (because he is the only one they can think of when asked and they did once have one of his Blue Periods in the cloakroom).

The following statistics are printed by courtesy of *Fur and Feather* (a magazine mainly devoted to Upper Class ceremonial attire). The average Middle Class adult goes to a concert 2.7 times a year, to the theatre 3.4 times, reads 9 books halfway through, and has never bought an original painting.

Food

The food situation has become increasingly confused by the easy availability of things like woodcocks and winkles.

The rising cost of everything has also helped to break down class barriers. Now that fish-and-chips are an expensive item carrying VAT they may be eaten without shame and in public view. Dietary pre-occupations have confused matters even more. One can refuse high-class food for health reasons and then eat cabbage on the same grounds. As a very loose guide, the Upper Class eat their food plain, the Middle Class grill it and the Lower Class fry it.

Food is a luxury whereas drink is a necessity. Admittedly drink is a very fluid subject and difficult to pin down. One could easily get out of one's depth. Many drinks that used to be very Upper Class have lost status through their introduction to the Lower classes during the War. At one time you might automatically have thought of champagne as an exclusively Upper Class drink. In fact, the Upper Class don't drink it with greater frequency than anyone else, but generally in greater quantities when they do. The only people who drink champagne regularly for nourishment are musical comedy actresses (traditionally out of shoes) and they only become Upper Class by marriage, which is not quite the same thing.

The only truly Upper Class drink remaining, is port. This they imbibe in huge quantities. Others may affect its use in Clubs etc., but they can never drink it with the flair of the true Upper Class alcoholic. A good malt whisky is both Upper Class and Middle Class (at least down to Middle Middle Class level) but blended whiskies confer no standing at all. Irish whiskey, in spite of expensive advertising, is still only drunk by the Irish. Vodka is now hugely imbibed by the Lower Class. Gin is liked by fast Lower Class ladies anxious to impress, by Middle Class ladies with tonic or bitter lemon and by Upper Class ladies with more gin. Brandy ought to rate higher than it does. It could be Upper Class to drink brandy all day starting at breakfast but its Middle Class use is so common now that it confers only financial distinction according to the number of stars on the bottle.

Which brings us to wine, the Lower Class drink of France, but still Middle Class in Britain. The unfashionable Middles buy their wine at Sainsbury's and then decant it so that nobody will see the label, but the fashionable Middle Class would be unhappy if their guests could not or did not bother to read the labels right down to the small print. Wine can only be Upper Class collectively, i.e. in the possession of a wine cellar, but even this doesn't count if the bottles are not dusty. Nowadays there is much more snobbery attached to beer: Middle Class snobbery on the whole, unless you have your own brewery like some Scottish manors do. The Lower Class drink anything that calls itself beer, but a good Middle Class drinker knows his Real Ale and bandies the names of obscure country breweries around. He will always demand that it be served to him in a straight glass. The nobbly glass with a handle reminds him too much of the days when he too used to drink anything. Cider is Lower Class and so is shandy, but Lager is vaguely Middle Class.

There would be a good case for claiming that tea is the most classless drink of all, except for Earl Grey which is a distinctly Upper Class brew. But coffee is very Middle Class, and even Lower Class. The Upper Class can take it or leave it.

Sport

The British of all classes are obsessed with sport and games and tend to judge the state that the country is in by its international successes in the sporting arena. When England (or one of the other home countries) wins, the Union Jack flies proudly and the stock market booms. At least 50 per cent of British conversation (at least amongst men) is on the subject of sport which, having a class structure that is a faithful reflection of the social structure, offers one of the most reliable barometers of class that we have.

Generally speaking fun which involves horses can be taken as Upper Class though, as in most things today, the demarcation lines are becoming a bit indistinct. However **Polo** is definitely Upper Class as you have to own several ponies, and be on speaking terms with the Royal Family. In addition polo grounds which are few and far between are firmly in the hands of the gentry. A certain amount of cheating goes on as teams that lack titled members of sufficient nerve and talent are known to import professionals from South America who look suitably wealthy and aristocratic when in action.

Hunting is the name given to the love of killing and is mainly distributed between Upper Class and Lower Class. The Middle Class are inclined to be a bit squeamish but are prepared to muscle in on the fox-hunting scene a bit for the prestige. Its availability is limited by the need to have a very large number of dogs (hounds) and horses big enough to jump over five-barred gates. The sport is run by the Upper Class but they allow the Middle Class to participate to get a good turn-out. Only the Upper Class could persuade farmers to let them gallop all over their land in return for an occasional sherry at the manor-house. The overwhelming majority of the public who do not want to exterminate animals, tolerate the sport because a) there is an equal chance of one of the huntsmen getting killed and b) hunting scenes look good on Christmas cards.

Deer-hunting is very Upper Class because they are the only people to have the requisite number of disposable deer, guns, gillies, etc. The Upper Class call it stalking, in case they miss.

Shooting birds is Upper Class if it involves land-based birds such as grouse and partridges. Those involved either know someone or have access to vast tracks of land. It needs armies of retainers, lodges, lavish picnic baskets and peasants willing to take the risk of being shot by mistake. It is now illegal to eat quail's eggs but the Upper Class do somehow still manage to have them for breakfast by dint of having their own quails. It is, however, Middle Class, or even Lower Class, to shoot water-birds such as geese and various kinds of duck because all that is needed is an inaccurate gun and an imitation duck with which the real duck stupidly tries to mate before it realises its mistake.

Fishing of course, is another matter. The whole sport, at least at Lower Class level, is a very passive affair. You don't actually hunt, chase or stalk a fish. It comes along and attaches itself to a line. Fishing is therefore indulged in by all classes, class differentiation depending on where it is done. The Lower Class fish in polluted rivers and reservoirs where what they catch is largely inedible. The Middle Class fish in private lakes and public ponds. The Upper Class own or hire river rights for salmon and trout. It is they who make it more of a sport by actually chasing their prey in the water.

Horse-racing is an area in which classes cross blend in all ways except function. Horses tend to be owned and bred by Upper Class and wealthy Middle Class imitators, but they are groomed and ridden mainly by the Lower Class. Race-meetings are, surprisingly, mainly attended by the Lower Class, who are there not to admire the races but to have what is colloquially known as a flutter. The Upper Class and Middle Class have flutters as well but tend to do it over the telephone. The Upper Class go to race-meetings to be seen. They are fenced off in small enclosures so that they will not get jostled by the Lower Class, but only by each other. Members of the Royal Family will often be observed, closely guarded by the Upper Class, in the middle of these enclosures. The Lower Middle Class only show an interest in two races – the Derby and the Grand National. Winning Upper Class owners are quaintly paid in guineas; all other punters get grubby banknotes.

Horse-jumping involves class in a different pattern. Horses that jump are owned mainly by the Upper Class or Upper Middle Class but even this area has been extended to owners and breeders in the Middle Class and Lower Class brackets. Upper Class riders can be distinguished in action – by the better fit of their riding clothes and by their hyphenated or distinctly Upper Class names. The Upper Class and Middle Class involvement in this sport is a natural extension of the junior obsession to jump over things on horses exhibited by Upper Class and Middle Class offspring. They prefer not to enter horse-races (all that mingling with Irish jockeys) and risk falling off their steeds in front of the Lower Class, and choose the horse-jumping arena where they can fall off in front of their equals or betters without loss of face.

Spectators at horse-jumping occasions are almost entirely Middle Class upwards. The terrible boredom of dressage events could only be endured by those who have an insatiable love of the horse.

The Upper Class, with rare exceptions, do not indulge in any sport on an active or professional level which involves baring the knees and other parts of the body. It is an interesting medical fact that the Upper Class very rarely seem to exhibit a good physical shape. Their legs and arms are generally flabby and thin and many suffer from curvature of the spine and stomach. If forced into shorts they prefer them to be at least knee-length. The Middle Class are far more shapely, with well-formed legs which they quite like showing off in briefer attire ranging from Upper Middle Class (four inches above the knees) Middle Middle Class (mid-thigh) and Lower Middle Class (just covering the bottom). Only Lower Class types are really well-built and muscular. No Upper Class person would dream of being muscular.

Athletics though mainly participated in by Lower Class who have naturally inherited the ability to run faster as they were always the ones being chased (e.g. poachers) also attracts some middle-class participants (mainly in the mile and more protracted events) and an occasional Lord. The curious part is that it has remained superficially (though not actually) amateur, on an expenses-only basis. Because of this it is watched with keen interest by all classes.

Cricket started out as a fairly highclass affair played on country pitches owned by squires. However, as the Upper Class could not (unaided) produce the prowess necessary for the satisfactory conclusion of the match – or the physique – they had to bring in Middle

Class and even Lower Class participants (Blacksmiths, for instance, always seemed to make the best fast-bowlers). Cricket was consequently saddled, until comparatively recent times, with a flagrant distinction: Players (Lower Class paid experts), and Gentlemen (Middle and Upper Class amateurs with flair), who entered the same changing-room through different doors. Cricket captains on the Army principle were drawn from the ranks of the Gentlemen and a fine old stir was caused when a Player was first chosen to lead England under a Labour government. Cricket is still run from an exclusive club in London and, regrettably, at least to readers of the *Telegraph*, has had to bow to winds of change and become partially Middle Class, which is why of course, the ruling body is known as the M.C.C. (Middle-Class-Cricket).

Golf was originally intended to be an Upper Class game; a simple healthy adjunct to Club life and a help in working off the effects of excessive food and drink. It was soon found, unfortunately, that Lower Class aides, caddies, greenkeepers, etc., had become so good at it that they had to be allowed to play on a professional basis. Later, because of the expensive upkeep of vast acres, the Middle Class had to be admitted as well. Class distinction is carefully maintained by clothing instead.

Tennis was invented by Henry VIII in the complicated early form still referred to as Real Tennis as if the present one was an hallucination. Owing to Henry's shape it was never intended to be a very active game and for years was played gently by the Upper Class hampered by long trousers and blazers (in the case of the ladies, long skirts) and was simply a matter of gently knocking a sponge to and fro over a strawberry net.

The intrusion of the Lower Class meant that the game acquired rules and a properly marked court. Tennis garb, for what now became an active and vicious sport, gradually dwindled until it could no longer decently become shorter. Even the socks have disappeared. Colonials and foreigners became so good at playing that the only ploy left to the British was to insist on competitions being held on grass. Even this failed. A stubborn rear-guard action was fought to keep it all in the gentleman and amateur orbit but not so long ago it became professional and eventually a part of show-business.

Boxing is only indulged in by the Upper Class and Middle Class in a very casual way, with a pact not to hit too hard. Participants in the commercial sport are firmly Lower Lower Class and rarely intellectual. The whole set-up from promoters down is run at a Lower Class level. The audiences are also predominantly Lower Class, and apparently demented, with a few Middle Class personages to be found in the expensive seats. The Upper Class organise their own bouts in what are euphemistically called Sporting Clubs where elderly gentleman, their white shirt fronts spattered with blood, enjoy watching young Lower Class athletes lose their residual brains. A sort of quaint survival of bear-baiting and cock-fighting.

Wrestling, except occasionally on a very amateur basis, is exclusively run and indulged in by Lower Class individuals, some so large that they count as two. Unlike boxing, the sport is arranged so that no-one actually hurts his opponent, although some sustain accidental injury when they trip over or fall out of the ring. It really belongs in the category of acting rather than sport. Because of the excitement of so much quivering flesh it is greatly enjoyed by Middle

Class and Upper Class ladies and elderly men of all classes who watch it avidly on television as an outlet for sexual frustration.

Rugger was created for Upper Class/Middle Class public school boys as a safety valve for cloistered emotions. It remained in that bracket for many years and was played by grammar-schools that wanted to give an impression of superiority to those who opted for soccer. A game of unredeemed violence and the spirit that both won and lost the Empire, it has all the inbuilt elements of appeal for the Middle Middle Class. It is also supported and played by the Upper Class whose ingrained love of violence and boredom is exhibited in a remote ancestor of rugby known as the Eton Wall Game. Unfortunately it became apparent that Lower Class louts were as good if not better at rugger and that Lower Class spectators were becoming more sophisticated and developing a liking for violence, boredom, the spirit that both won and lost the Empire, etc. Wisely, for once, rather than let it complicate the game (as in cricket) the Upper Class/Middle Class version (known as Rugby Union for some obscure reason) remained unsullied, and a slightly cleaner version, in which the player was allowed to get rid of the ball on a voluntary basis (known as Rugby League) was set aside for the Lower Class.

As most of the Lower Class and some Lower Middle Class remained obdurately unmoved by Rugger a new game involving skill was invented called Association Football or **Soccer**. The big difference was that instead of kicking your opponent, you kick the ball. At last the Lower Class and Lower Middle Class had a game that was exclusively their own, to be watched, played and even administered by their own kind. The only occasion when the Upper Class gets involved is when one of them is produced to hand over the Cup at Wembley. This is because the ground on which Wembley stadium stands was once part of the Empire.

Then there is **Squash**; not really a sport, more an endurance test. The participants are locked in a small room and hit a small hard rubber ball at the walls and each other. A hit on the buttocks results in a red mark being awarded. It is played at an amateur level by Middle Class keep-fit addicts and professionally by large muscular Lower Class Australians, small muscular classless Pakistanis and one muscular English man.

Billiards and Snooker should not actually be lumped together although both began as Upper Class games played in Indian clubs and Upper Class homes that had spare and sufficient space for them. Billiards, now only played by the over seventies, went out before it could be properly commercialised. Snooker, played by all on an amateur basis, is played by Lower Class professionals with an absurdly high level of skill, and has now become a sport.

EVENTS OF THE YEAR

Upper Class: Ascot. The glorious 12th. Badminton Horse Trials. The Garden Party. The broaching of the port laid down fifty years ago. Croquet. Bath night.

Middle Class: The Derby. Brands Hatch. The Tests. Wedding anniversaries. Renewal of multifarious licences. The Boat Race. Crufts. Wimbledon. The Club AGM.

Lower Class: The Grand National. The Cup Final. Christmas. Mother's Day. Pay Day.

GLOSSARY

Bogus titles – Titles which are conferred by foreign countries and therefore have no validity in Great Britain. You must not be fooled into the belief that the bearer thereof is a gentleman or lady. For example, anyone introducing themselves as the Archduke Ferdinand or the Countess Maritza should immediately be suspect. A Baron could also be a foreign upstart with no real standing except the possession of a lot of money. Be tactful here. A Baronet on the other hand is a Sir with an insurance policy and should be treated respectfully. It might also be noted that many people who call themselves Sir, Lord, Earl, Duke (even King), and so-on, are simply jazz musicians and decidedly Lower Class.

Ethnic minorites – Small groups of nationals who find themselves in a situation of isolation within communities of another race, e.g. the English in London.

Honours List – A system of good behaviour awards given by the Upper Class to the Middle Class to make them happy and subservient. Today some are even given, as a broad-minded gesture, to Lower Class people like musicians and footballers and pop stars. It has been a valuable inhibitor of revolutionary tendencies. Give a bolshevist an MBE and he immediately loses conviction.

Institute of Directors – A gathering of wealthy business men who agree (over packed lunches and champagne) that there should be no unions, bank-holidays, wage rises, health service, charity of any sort, or Lower Class membership of golf clubs.

Jobs for the Boys – A valuable system of preferment which ensures that the various classes do not get assigned to the wrong areas of employment.

Slumming – Deliberately trying to appear to be a class or two lower than one is, either for the fun of it, or for propaganda purposes. Most frequently indulged in by rich or titled Socialist politicians. Occasionally, for short periods, by high-ranking clergy. It carries curiously mixed and ambiguous overtones, however, as he that slummeth, although appearing to do it with the humblest and sincerest of motives, would still like you to know that he is doing it and really belongs to a higher class – otherwise there would be no point in doing it at all.

Snob, snobbery, snobbish – A Lower Class person will refer to anyone of Middle Class or Upper Class status as a snob and really mean it. Middle Class people are not so presumptuous as to refer to the Upper Class as snobs but rather to one of their own class who thinks he is. It is interesting to note that the original eighteenth century meaning of the word was: *One who belongs to the lower classes without pretentions to rank or gentility; a cobbler.*

Stiff upper lip – A condition brought about by an excess of good manners and a genuine attempt not to sneer when talking of the Lower Classes. Over the centuries the upper lip was thus rendered rigid. The phenomenon was also associated with the concealment of fear, tears, and other such weakling emotions, cf. Shakespeare: *'Verily, a brave fellow with a lip as stiff as a muller's poker.'*

THE AUTHOR

Of proud Lower Middle Class origins, Peter Gammond is able to trace his ancestry on the paternal side back to a Herefordshire byre-sweeper, and on the maternal side to a medieval Cheshire mud-wrestler. Before that there was a rarely mentioned French connection which has resulted in a reactionary inability to speak the language.

Through inter-marriage in Printing, Publishing and the Law, he now presides over a superficially Lower Middle Class family with Upper Lower Class undertones only betrayed by musical interests. He has also known the privations of not being able to afford malt whisky and half-coronas, but now maintains a respectable image by membership of a semi-respectable London club, playing artisan golf, and living on the fringes of the stockbroker belt in Surrey.

Peter Gammond carefully hides his profession of author under such categorisations as publisher and broadcaster, and any suspicion of musical talent by a controlled display of inefficiency. He is proud that his two sons have remained Lower Class, one as a working journalist, and the other as an unemployed film director. Both have a profound interest in soccer, pop music and like chips with everything. In his own right he has acquired various Middle Middle Class traits, which his offspring deplore, such as a fearful respect for authority, the wearing of a tie at christenings, marriages and Rotary meetings, and a liking for the poetry of John Betjeman and the novels of Evelyn Waugh. He is unable to hide the revealing fact that he has written and published some thirty books, though not always on a fully professional basis.